Machu Picchu: Virtual Guide and Secrets Revealed

Copyright Brien Foerster 2012

Cover art copyright Lewis Adams 2012

All photos and drawings other than those of the author are deemed to be copyright free; any exceptions were purely accidental.

Dedication

First and foremost, I thank the Inca people for having constructed such ingenious and phenomenally well made works of megalithic form and function. The quality of their achievements in stone are as strong and meaningful I believe today as the more than 500 years that have passed since the last of their great works. The Inca were not simply great builders, they were also the caretakers of the people and lands that they oversaw, not ruled; a population that may have been as high as 15,000,000 souls at the time of European "contact."

That the language of the Inca survives, Runa Simi, also known as Quechua, and is spoke by millions of mainly Native Peruvians and Bolivians, as do the forms of dance and other arts, is a testament to an incredibly strong people. Though the Spanish soldiers of fortune, romantically named "conquistadors" by themselves for their own gratification, crushed the Inca nobility and people with such horrific malice and cruelty, along with many other native cultures, they could not bruise or even touch the peoples' souls, nor their will to persevere and thrive.

Machu Picchu stands triumphantly on top of a mountain of the same name, lush with vegetation, and is visited by at least 2000 people from around the world every day, a symbol of the aesthetic, engineering and imagination of a people of genius. May it always do so.

My thanks to Graham Hancock for allowing me to write columns for his website, and for supporting my first book: **A Brief History Of The Incas; From Rise, Through Reign To Ruin** by making me author of the month. To my Ancestors, who have guided me this far, and to my dear Irene, keeper of my heart.

Chapters

1/ Introduction

2/ Birth Of The Inca

3/ The Discovery Of Machu Picchu

4/ Who Built Machu Picchu And Why?

5/ Why Was Machu Picchu Abandoned?

6/ The Virtual Tour

1/ Introduction

Atop a lofty mountain, on the edge of the Amazon rainforest in Peru, lie the ruins of a once proud city known to the world as Machu Picchu. In 2010 it was listed as "One of the Seven Wonders of the World" by UNESCO, and since then its fame and popularity have increased even further than before. On average, 2000 people per day, 365 days a year visit this place, drawn by it's exotic location, and the fact that it is reported as being the only Inca site of any size that the Spanish, under the conquistador Francisco Pizarro, never found, and thus never plundered for it's gold.

But what is the real story of this place? Who built it, when, why, and what explains its popularity to visitors from all over the world? To answer this, we must, as an honest gesture, balance our inquiry. Most so-called "ruins" of ancient cultures, and the term "ruin" seems to automatically put into the mind of the reader abandoned structures with crumbling stone walls, are the domain of study by university trained academics; archaeologists and anthropologists. They tend to analyze what the inhabitants left behind; pot shards, fire pits, writings (if any) and the buildings, etc.

What they tend not to do is ask the descendants of the presumed makers of the structures the nature of who the ancestors were, and accounts of their origins, accomplishments, and reasons for their demise. By adding both of these types of exploration together, the reader may achieve what may well be a much fuller understanding of, in this case Machu Picchu and the Inca people who built it, than they would from a purely western scientific approach, or one based solely on oral traditions. And believe me, the latter is much more difficult to obtain than the former, in most cases.

For some reason, and I frankly call it cultural arrogance that many if not most western academics and writers never consult Indigenous people in regards to the constructions and people of the past. For example, the Mayan calendar, and the year 2012. Millions of dollars have been made by many writers on this subject, and the most common theme, as well as outcome of their treatise is that the world ends on December 21, 2012, in a series of natural as well as perhaps human made disasters. But what do the oral traditions of the Maya themselves say on the subject? The wisdom keepers of the traditions whom I have heard or spoken to say the same thing; a world ends on that date; not THE world, but "a world," which is a term they use for an age, a period of time. And what happens after that? A new "world" or age begins.

Machu Picchu is a similar situation in some ways. The majority of books written about it limit their knowledge and focus to archaeological work done since Hiram Bingham III, the American explorer stumbled across it in 1911, frankly looking for another site altogether. They know that it was built during the time of Pachacutec, the 9th Sapa (ruling) Inca, but rarely if ever entertain the idea, which some stone structures will show you in this book, that earlier builders were there as well. Oral traditions, still alive and well in Cusco, but rarely put to paper, especially in English, also tell a much richer and older story.

At the outset, I wish to frankly state that this is not the "be all and end all" Machu Picchu book. I wrote it for the visitor, who wishes to walk through this breath taking landscape and learn more in about 100 pages than what, frankly, most tour guides offer. Also, it is for those that will never see this amazing place for themselves, due to lack of finances, fear of travel, or infirmity. I have made it my quest, after many trips to Machu Picchu to present you with what may be best regarded as a virtual guide, rather than an epic tome on the subject.

What I wish to present is as balanced a story as possible, presenting both archaeological discoveries as well as the oral traditions. So let us start with the Inca themselves, the makers of the majority of what is found at Machu Picchu. Who were they, and where did they come from?

2/ Birth Of The Inca

The oral traditions vary to some degree, as does the archaeological evidence. But, the general belief is that the Inca are from the area, to the south, at or near Lake Titicaca. The most common story is that the Inca "rose from Lake Titicaca," summoned by their creator God Viracocha; who was the energy behind the creation of all things. The sun is often written of as having been this main deity, but in fact the sun, known as Inti in the Runa simi or Quechua language, was more likely the physical manifestation of Viracocha. Inti was thus a symbol, in real life, that the Inca could observe on a daily basis, much like, perhaps, the cross is a physical symbol of Jesus.

The two founding Inca were Manco Capac, and his sister and wife, Mama Ocllo. They were told by their creator Viracocha to leave the area of Lake Titicaca and found a new civilization. But this, in reality is hardly the whole picture. Manco Capac was most likely the leader of a group of people, perhaps an extended family or clan. Many of the oral traditions speak of there having being four brothers, with the surname Ayar, they being Ayar Manco (known later as Manco Capac once he assumed power), Ayar Anca, Ayar Cachi, and Ayar Uchu. As well, there were three sisters of Mama Occlo, they were Mama Huaco, Mama Cura (or Ipacura), and Mama Raua. These three sisters, and three brothers, are said to have also been married, very much an Inca behaviour, as bloodlines and social position were an enduring concept throughout the Inca civilization, from beginning to the end.

Some traditions speak of these first Inca as having come from a place called Pacaritambo in the Sacred Valley area outside of Cusco, but the more famous stories say that they came from Lake Titicaca, sometimes literally, and other times symbolically.

VERY fanciful portrayal of Manco Capac and Mama Occlo

The two most probable candidates for the homeland of the Inca, near Lake Titicaca, are the Island of the Sun, located in the lake, and presently part of Bolivia, or Tiwanaku (Tiahuanaco) which is approximately 11 km. south of the lake. I have been to the Island of the Sun, and was frankly disappointed with the lack of Inca period ruins there. So, it seems improbable to me that this was their homeland. However, oral traditions to say that most of the Inca buildings that did existed at the time of the arrival of the Spanish in Cusco, in 1533, were dismantled by the Inca, and all gold and silver ornaments and sculptures were thrown into the lake, in order that the Spanish couldn't take them. Whether this is true or not, I have not been able to find out. However, there still exist vast agricultural terraces, called Andene on the island, dating back to at least Inca times which could have easily fed quite a large population of people.

The nearby Island Of The Moon is thought by some to be another candidate as the Inca homeland, but is small, and could not host a large population. Even if there is some evidence of an Inca presence on either or both of these islands prior to their moving to Cusco, where they came prior to that has not been answered as far as I know.

Inca stairway at the south end of the Island of the Sun

The other candidate is Tiwanaku, which still has many finely crafted stone walls, which are believed to be the hallmarks of the Inca. Tiwanaku, according to conventional scholarship, began at approximately 300 BC, and was abandoned about 900 AD due to climate change; the area experienced a 40 year El Nino influenced drought, and this so weakened the last of the surviving people, that they were forced to leave. Also, as a result of this weakness, local Aymara language speaking tribal people attacked the people of Tiwanaku.

Even in its present somewhat dilapidated state, Tiwanaku shows us that its people were master stone masons and very spiritually minded.

The basic layout of what Tiwanaku would have looked like.

A seven level pyramid and ceremonial courtyard welcome visitors to this day. The actual construction techniques employed here are similar in style and execution to some of those seen in Cusco and the Sacred Valley of Peru, and this is the strongest evidence that the Inca came from here. Also, in terms of timing, the collapse of Tiwanaku about 900 AD fits in with the theory that the Inca first arrived in Cusco and the Sacred Valley in or around the 12th century. Going back to our story, the creator God Viracocha told the first Inca, Manco Capac and Mama Ocllo to go forth, with a golden staff, and found what turned out to be Cusco.

The fact that Manco Capac and Mama Ocllo are written of as being wedded brother and sister was not a one time event. As was touched on earlier, it was the practice of the Inca, from their beginnings, and through until their destruction by the Spanish commencing in 1532, that the sapa (High) ruling Inca marry his sister. It is believed by many sources that the term "sister" may have included direct cousins; in any event, it was important to the Inca that their royal, and in fact "divine" blood line be maintained in as pure a fashion as possible.

Comic like depiction of the arrival of the Inca in Cusco

The reasoning behind this practice was that the Inca were "Children Of The Sun," believing that they were direct descendants of the sun god Inti. However, as I have stated earlier, it is more probable that Inti, was used to symbolize the creator God Viracocha. As direct descendants of the divine, the purity of their bloodline was vital to the purity of their quest; to "civilize" all those that they came in contact with. Again, they are believed to have arrived in Cusco and the Sacred Valley about 1200 AD. At that time, there were at least 3 native groups living in Cusco; the Sawasiray, Allkawisas, and the Maras. It is believed that the Inca, who of course numbered more than just Manco Capac and Mama Ocllo, did not have to subdue these people with military force, but simply awed them with their vast knowledge of the "civilized" arts, including metallurgy, laws of ethical conduct, warfare, agricultural terrace construction, and other forms of engineering and building with stone.

This then was the beginning of Inca Cusco. From this time on there were a total of 12 sapa Inca, as follows:

Manco Capac   1200-1230

Sinchi Roca   1230-1260

LloqueYupanqui   1260-1290

Mayta Capac   1290-1320

Capac Yupanqui   1320-1350

Inca Roca   1350-1380

Yahuar Huacac   1380-1410

Viracocha   1410-1438

Pachacutec   1438 – 1471

Tupac Inca Yupanqui 1471 – 1493

Huayna Capac   1493 – 1527

Ninan Cuyochi   1527

Huascar	1527 – 1532
Atahualpa	1532 – 1533

During the 14th century, the leaders Sinchi Roca, Lloki Yupanqui, Mayta Capa, and Capac Yupanqui supposedly led several wars against neighbouring tribes of Cusco. By the time that Capac Yupanqui died, Inca Roca had gained enough power to become Hanan, and thus controlled all aspects of political, religious, and military affairs. However, it is also possible that these "wars" were fabrications of Spanish authors.

After Inca Roca's death, the Inca state began to decline under the rule of Yahuar Huacac. However, the next Sapa Inca, Viracocha, stabilized the state, which now reached a 50 km radius from Cusco. At this time the Chanka tribe had expanded its territories south of Cusco, and along with an alliance of other southern tribes, made a move to attack Cusco. The Chanka army greatly outnumbered that of the Inca, and as the battle started, the Chanka placed a statue of their founder in front of their troops. During the battle, the Inca took control of the statue, and perhaps seeing this as a terrible omen, the Chanka deserted the battlefield.

The next Sapa Inca, Pachacuti, whose name roughly translates as " Earth Shaker " began the great expansion period of the confederation. During his reign, he and his son, Tupac Inca Yupanqui brought much of the Andes, roughly modern day Peru and Ecuador, under Inca control. The areas to the south, as in what is now called Chile, were enveloped into the Inca sphere of influence, the so called "empire" by previous Inca leaders.

Stylized painting of the Sapa Inca Pachacutec

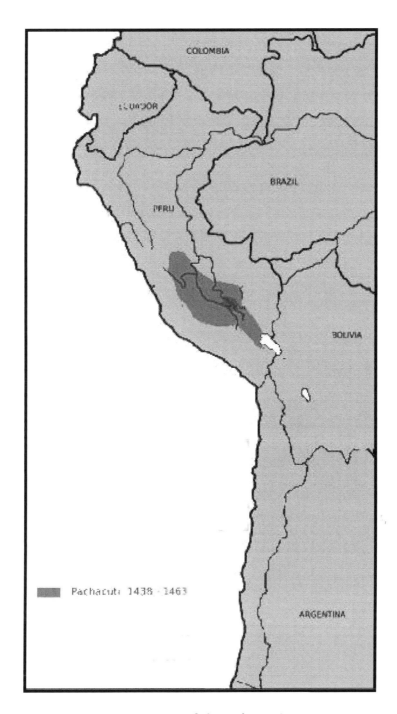

Early expansion of the Tahuantinsuyu

Pachacutec was the founder of the Tahuantinsuyu; a federalist system which consisted of a central government with the Sapa Inca at its head, in Cusco, and four provincial governments with strong leaders: Chinchsuyu (NW), Antisuyu (NE), Contisuyu (SW), and

Collasuyu (SE.) Pachacutec is also regarded as the builder of Machu Picchu. What sets the Inca's method of territorial expansion at this time, and perhaps earlier, from other cultures is both intriguing and very clever. They formed a confederation, not an empire, and this point can not be emphasized enough. Empires tend to grow based on the subjugation and destruction of other groups and nations; not only their political systems and military, but also their belief systems. A confederation is an alliance of groups and or nations.

Pachacutec sent spies to regions that he wanted to expand into. These spies brought back reports on the political organization, military might, and wealth of the prospective confederation candidates. He would then send messages to the leaders of these lands extolling the benefits of joining the confederation, offering them presents of luxury goods such as high quality textiles. Benefits to the candidate lands included access to the extensive Inca road system, some 15000 to 25000 miles in size, and the goods and services that were within the realm of the Inca's sphere of influence.The benefits to the Inca were access to goods and services that were particular to that region.

Most accepted the rule of the Inca, and acquiesced peacefully. It was only when a perspective Candidate refused to join the confederation that military force was used. This was the case in only three cases that I have found, and those were the Chanka from the nearby Apurimac region, the Chimu people in the north of Peru, near present day Trujillo, and the Chachapoya, known as the "Warriors of the Clouds" who lived on the edge of the Amazon jungle area east of Cajamarca.

It was traditional for the Inca's first born son to lead the army, and from the time of Manco Capac to Huayna Capac the first born son inherited the title of Sapa Inca. Pachacutec's son Tupac Inca began conquests to the north in 1463, and continued them as Inca after Pachacutec's death in 1471. His most important "conquest " was the kingdom of Chimor (Chan chan is a remnant of that culture) the Inca's only serious rival on the north coast of Peru. Tupac Inca then expanded into modern day Ecuador and Colombia.

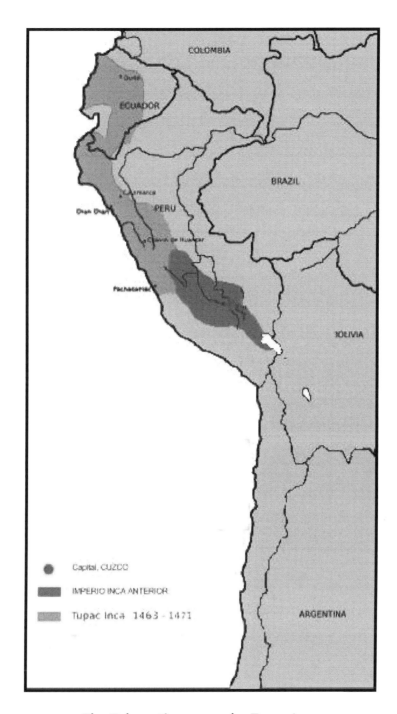

The Tahuantinsuyu under Tupac Inca

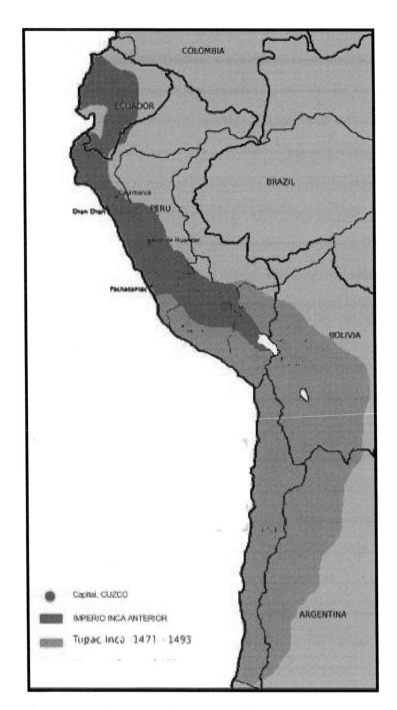

Tahuantinsuyu by the time of Pachacutec

Tupac's son, Huayna Capac, added significant territory to the south. At its height, Tahuantinsuyu included Peru and Bolivia, most of what is now Ecuador, a large portion of what is today northern Chile (as far south as Santiago) and extended into corners of

Argentina and Colombia. At this time, Tahuantinsuyu was the largest confederation or empire in the pre-Columbian Americas.

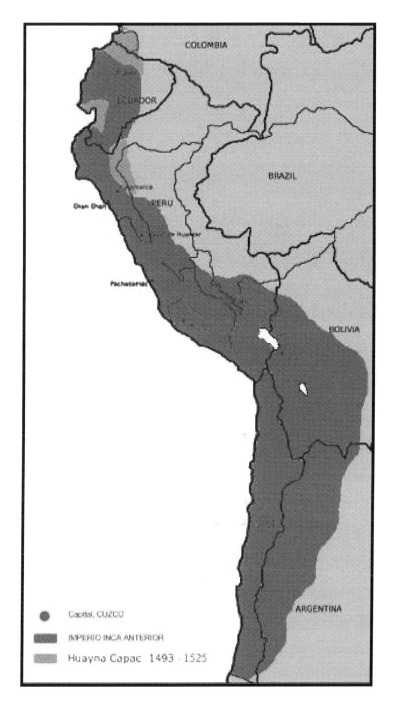

The eclipse of the Tahuantinsuyu with Huayna Capac

Huayna Capac spent his later years in Quito, Ecuador, where his Ecuadorian wife (his principal wife, or Qoya, lived in Cusco and was the mother of Ninan Cuyochi and Huascar) bore him a son, Atahualpa. Huayna Capac died in 1527, supposedly from small pox which had made its way through the native communities from Panama, and Ninan Cuyochi then became the Sapa Inca, as he was the first-born son. Ninan Cuyochi was, however, Sapa Inca for only a year, as he too succumbed to small pox. It is possible that Huayna Capac knew that Ninan Cuyochi's reign would be short, and he supposedly declared that Huascar and Atahualpa should share power, a definite break in the previous arrangement of passing the title of Sapa Inca from father to first born son.

In 1527, after the death of Ninan Cuyochi, Atalhualpa became sovereign of the ancient kingdom of Quito, and Huascar was given the rest of the Tahuantinsuyu. Civil war broke out between the two brothers at some point between 1527 and 1532. Huascar was eventually captured by Atahualpa in 1532 and executed. Atahualpa became Sapa Inca for only a period of months, when he in turn was executed by the Spanish in 1533, having arrived on the Peruvian shores a year previously.

The death of Ninan Cuyochi ended the traditional rite of Sapa Inca succession, as I stated above. With the death of Huascar and Atahualpa, the Tahuantinsuyu fell into a state of disarray, and the confederation began to crumble. In order to restore some sort of order, the Spanish installed Manco Inca Yupanqui, the younger brother of Huascar (from a different and lesser Cusquean mother) as Sapa Inca;in essence a puppet Sapa Inca. A feud developed amongst the Spanish; Pizarro, the Spanish leader, was fighting resistance and tribal separation to the north of Cusco, while his associate Diego de Amagro decided to claim Cusco as his own property. Yupanqui decided to use this intra-spanish feud to his advantage, recapturing Cusco in 1536, but the Spanish soon retook the city.

Manco Inca Yupanqui then retreated to the mountain retreat of Vilcabamba, close to Machu Picchu, where he and his followers remained for another 36 years, sometimes raiding the Spanish or inciting revolts against them. In 1572 this last Inca stronghold was discovered, and Tupac Amaru, Manco's son, was captured and executed, bringing the great Inca confederation and civilization to an end. Without the Sapa Inca being present as the political, religious, and military figurehead and center of power, it made it relatively easy for the Spanish to seize control of the masses of Peruvian people; a position that their descendants have even now in the twenty first century.

If the reader would like to learn more about the history of the Inca, and the "civil war" that occurred just prior to the arrival of the Spanish in 1532, please read my book: "**A Brief History Of The Incas: From Rise, Through Reign To Ruin**" available in paperback from http://www.adventuresunlimitedpress.com/proddetail.php?prod=BHOI&cat=36 and as an e-book through my website, www.hiddenincatours.com, and www.amazon.com, along with my other books.

3/ The Discovery Of Machu Picchu

In the April 1913 edition of National Geographic magazine, published in the United States, including a three page fold out photo, a young archaeologist named Hiram Bingham III, who was raised in Hawaii and descended from Christian missionaries, wrote an article about a lost Inca city that he had discovered in the Peruvian jungle. That "city" was of course Machu Picchu.

Today, there is a train named after this great explorer, which takes the visitor, in luxury, from the Inca town of Ollantaytambo, in the Sacred Valley near Cusco, to the small tourist village of Aguas Calientes, and back. From there, a 20 minute bus ride through several hair pin turns and over 1000 feet of vertical ascent takes you to the entrance to the "lost" city. This is not the only train that does this route every day; there are in fact 3 companies, travelling along the same stretch of track, which can take your there, but the Hiram Bingham run gives you free Champagne.

A lost city; forgotten in the tropical mountain jungle for about 400 years; Inca gold; danger, intrigue, heroism...wait a second...

How much of this is true, and how much is hype generated by the tourist industry and Peruvian government to get you to go there? A fair amount, in my opinion.

Machu Picchu is in fact the name of a mountain. In the indigenous language of the area, commonly called Quechua, Machu means old, and Picchu means bird or mountain. Hiram Bingham was actually looking for the last known refuge of the Inca, a site called old Vilcabamba, on the fringe of the Sacred Valley where it descends into the dense Amazon jungle. After finding some stone Inca ruins in the general area, such as the White Rock and Vitcos, a local Native person told him that similar structures could be found on the mountain called Machu Picchu.

The famous White Rock, or Yurac Rumi

4/ Who Built Machu Picchu And Why?

The most common tale of this majestic place was that it was abandoned by the Inca at the time of the Spanish conquest, around 1532 or so, and was lost to the world, becoming completely overgrown with jungle vegetation, until the "discovery" by Bingham in 1911.

Most guides, and academic publications, will tell you that Machu Picchu was simply a jungle clad mountain top prior to the reign of Pachacutec, and it was under his instruction that the whole complex was built between 1438 and 1472, and some assert that it was completed within an even narrower time frame. Theories vary as to its function prior to abandonment, from royal estate, to religious sanctuary, a settlement built to control the economy of conquered regions, a prison for a select few who had committed heinous crimes against Inca society, or even an agricultural experimentation, like Moray, shown below.

The agricultural experimental station of Moray, near Cusco

Moray (also spelled Merey) is perhaps the finest example of the Inca's expertise at agricultural experimentation. It is said that each terrace acted as a microclimate whereby corn, potato, quinoa and other crops could be tested and cross bred to maximize the growing capacity of the Tahuantinsuyu. Since the population of people under Inca influence by the 16th century was at least 10,000,000 it was important to be able to grow the staple foods under as many climate conditions as possible.

View of Machu picchu from the end of the Inca Trail

The true story is most likely, as said earlier, both more interesting and complicated. Pachacutec was most likely the sapa (high) Inca who had the majority of Machu Picchu constructed, and made it a place where he could escape from Cusco, during the relatively cold of winter, and rejuvenate. But it was not his private domain, but more like the equivalent of the modern United States President's Camp David; a place where high officials and advisers from Cusco, and throughout the Tahuantinsuyu (Inca name for their civilization and territory) would meet to discuss the affairs of state, and be pampered in a beautiful mountain top spa like setting. Stretching from Colombia and Ecuador in the north to the middle of Chile in the south by the mid 15th century, the great size of the Tahuantinsuyu would have required a central meeting place for the military, spiritual, and political leaders of each region to meet and discuss current situations and future plans. Cusco, though it was the center as capital and geographic hub, may possibly have been too public a place for delicate affairs to be discussed. Thus, a location such as Machu Picchu, being located less than 100 km away from Cusco and with a more benign climate, would have been a perfect choice.

Only two roads, more like trails enter the citadel; one being the famous "Inca Trail" which hundreds of tourists use each day, and another on the north face gave access to Machu Picchu. This would have ensured that access was limited, and military sentries at these "choke points" would have deterred unwarranted intruders. It is possible that other routes did exist during Inca times, but due to the location of this masterpiece of engineering and construction, being on the edge of the Amazon jungle, fast growing foliage could easily have obscured any path no longer in use very rapidly.

The Inca Trail approaching Machu Picchu

The major traditional approach to Machu Picchu would have been the present day famous "Inca Trail" which is in fact a very short segment of the Inca road system, traditionally called the Qapaq Nan; Great Road. It is actually a small tributary that today leads from the town of Urubamba in the Sacred Valley to Machu Picchu itself. The original road originated in Cusco, and the present highway that connects Cusco and Urubamba was also part of this Inca Trail originally. Visitors today approach Machu Picchu by way of a "switch back" road, constructed in the early 20th century; an access for archaeological crews most likely created by Hiram Bingham. Other trails, secret even to this day most likely exist; on my third trip there my wife and I met a Qero shaman, the Qero being the last of the spiritual carriers of Inca wisdom who live in villages high on the mountain called Ausengate, told us that he had entered the area via a trail that only they know of.

Further back on the Inca Trail, with Machu Picchu in the distance

Contrary to popular belief, the Qero are not the blood descendants of the Inca; not true blooded at least. They are people of very small stature and Indigenous features, whereas the Inca were a distinct family of people, physically tall, possibly with dark red hair and supposedly exhibiting the remnants of cranial elongation. That is the subject of a book that I wrote with David Hatcher Childress called: **"The Enigma Of Cranial Deformation"**, available through www.adventuresunlimitedpress.com, and www.amazon.com.

View of Machu Picchu and the zig zag bus road to it

The original road is very narrow, and if not constantly maintained, as has been explained earlier, quickly becomes overgrown with tropical vegetation. This could also explain why the location of the site faded from local consciousness after it was abandoned; it would be easy for the jungle to quickly erase the road from view. The other well known access to Machu Picchu is a very narrow trail that hugs the side of the hills below it, and reaches the site on its north western side. The drawbridge that can still be viewed there adds further evidence that access to the area was highly restricted.

The alternate route to Machu Picchu with wooden draw bridge

The drawbridge base is made of roughly shaped stones, reasonably well fitted together, so this is most likely Inca construction, and not that of an earlier culture. Wooden planks stretched across and made a bridge in one section, cutting off access to Machu Picchu via this route if they were removed.

As has been said, Hiram Bingham was the first person to expose Machu Picchu to the world, through National Geographic Society sponsorship and exposure in their famed magazine; in fact, they devoted the entire April 1913 issue to Machu Picchu. But he hardly "discovered it." An American historian employed as a lecturer at Yale University, Bingham had been searching for the city of Vilcabamba, which was the last Inca refuge during the Spanish conquest. He had worked for years in previous trips and explorations around the zone, and it was Pablito Alvarez, a local 11 year-old local Quechua speaking Native boy, led Bingham up to Machu Picchu.

The site was not completely covered in vegetation as I have said. In fact, Bingham stumbled across two native farmers, named Richarte and Alvarez, who had cleared some of the Inca terraces and had been growing potatoes, corn, sugarcane and other crops there for 3 or 4 years, and were living there, possibly full time.

Also, other adventurers had been there before Bingham. . Simone Waisbard, a long-time researcher from Cusco, claims that Enrique Palma, Gabino Sánchez, and Agustín Lizárraga left their names engraved on one of the rocks at Machu Picchu on 14 July 1901. Also in 1904, an engineer named Franklin supposedly spotted the ruins from a distant mountain. He told Thomas Payne, an English Christian missionary living in the region, about the site, Payne's family members claim. They also report that in 1906, Payne and fellow missionary Stuart E. McNairn (1867–1956) climbed up to the ruins.

The site may have been discovered and plundered in 1867 by a German businessman, Augusto Berns. There is some evidence that a German engineer, J. M. von Hassel, arrived earlier. Maps found by historians show references to Machu Picchu as early as 1874.

Photo taken of Machu Picchu during the excavations by Hiram Bingham.

5/ Why Was Machu Picchu Abandoned?

And the question arises, why was Machu Picchu abandoned? The obvious answer is that the Spanish had arrived, and so this special place was left, en masse so that they would not find it. But that is too simple an answer. What is more probable is that it was the victim of introduced diseases, and the Inca civil war which had just preceded the Spanish conquest. Oral traditions indicate that Machu Picchu was, as well as being in a spa and resting place for the Inca and officials, also a medical experimental place.

It is said that the medical personnel there were using snake venom in order to cure diseases, and extend human life expectancy. This could of course be a fable, but the story is intriguing. What is said is that the officials who were staying at Machu Picchu at the time of the civil war between the full blood Inca Huascar, and the half-blood from Ecuador, Atahualpa, were on Huascar's side of the conflict, because he was the true leader.

Atahaullpa wished to conquer the entire Tahuantinsuyu, and wanted all full blood Inca, as well as Inca officials killed. Upon this news reaching Machu Picchu via the Inca runners, the Chasqui, all personnel decided to abandon the site. The evacuation is also said to be in conjunction with the fact that news had reached them of a mysterious group of humans who had just landed on the north coast near Tumbes, and brought death with them.

The diseases which became plagues had preceded the arrival of the Spanish, by moving through the Native populations from the north, starting in Panama, where the Spanish had an early settlement. Supposedly, the last act that the inhabitants performed, was the release of the poisonous snakes that they were keeping for experimental purposes. That could be the reason why the local people didn't necessarily forget about Machu Picchu's existence, they simply considered it a dangerous place. They only returned to the citadel en masse when Hiram Bingham showed up...with money to hire them to clear the area of jungle overgrowth. However, this was the past; let us now enter and explore this very special space. It has probably cost you 200 dollars for this day's outing, when taking into account the bus from Cusco, the train from Ollantaytambo to Aguas

Calientes, the entrance ticket, and then the bus to the site itself. I urge you to maximize your time here; too many of the guides that you can hire try to push you through too fast. This may be the only time you visit Machu Picchu, so make the effort and cost worth it.

Your first view of Machu Picchu beyond the tourist entrance

6/ The Virtual Tour

The above photo is what greets you once you enter through the main gate. The simplest way to see Machu Picchu is by making a clock wise route through the whole complex. This gate is not the traditional entrance as used by the Inca; you are actually entering onto the beginning of the main agricultural terrace (Andene) system, and the buildings here are thought to have been either workers houses, or where farming tools were stored, or perhaps both.

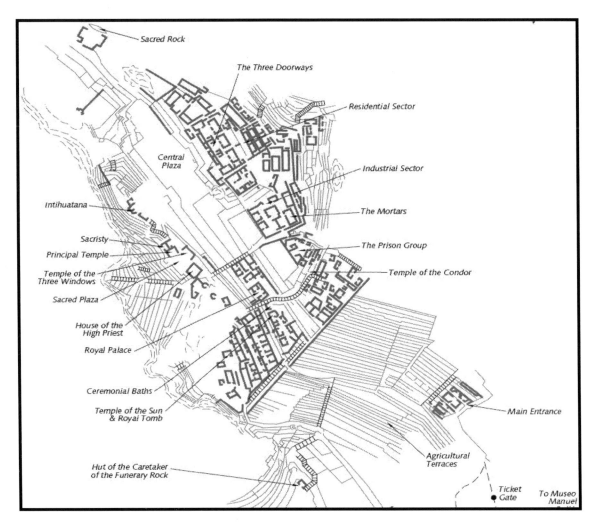

Diagram of the Machu picchu complex

The traditional entrance, via the Inca Trail, takes you into the city just below the "Hut of the Caretaker", which looms high above you to your left. Before we actually begin the tour, please take into account that many of the names and functions of buildings and spaces at Machu Picchu are speculation, based on the observations and thoughts mainly of Hiram Bingham, who is not believed to have consulted much with oral tradition experts. But then again, who could he have consulted with, as few people theoretically had knowledge of its existence since the 16th century. Some of the place names clearly ring true, such as Temple of the Condor and Intihuatana (Hitching Post of the Sun), but others, such as the Industrial Sector and Prison group are sheer guess work, and most probably untrue. No one has updated the place names since Bingham labelled them 100 years ago, which seems to me to be very careless.

Our tour may stray from the conventional one given by most guides, and in fact it already has, but it is based on melding oral and conventional histories together, as much as is possible. Unfortunately, in recent times the caretakers of Machu Picchu have set up a series, indeed a system of blue signs with arrows on them, trying to get you to follow a preset, clockwise course. This may have been done in order to make the 2000 plus visitors per day move through the site efficiently, but does restrict those of us who wish to probe more deeply. The average tourist is content with 3 hours wandering around, and with what the average tour guides says. But for those of us with more inquiring minds, a full day, at least, is the minimum.

Though the little blue signs urge you to take a particular path, to do so is not mandatory.

Looking up, left, at the "Hut Of The Caretaker"

Looking back at the entrance and gardeners' houses at Machu Picchu

We walk along the Inca made terraces to reach the first main set of stairs, which takes us up, and to the left. It is from here, near the "Hut of the Caretaker" that we get the first true view of the whole city. The agricultural terraces are clearly of Inca period construction; they were masters of this technology, brought from their homeland of Lake Titicaca, whose entire hillsides were sculpted to feed what would have been a very large population perhaps 1500 years ago, when Tiwanaku and other major centers were still in their prime.

The massive terracing system at Machu Picchu shows us that the site could have quite easily been self-sufficient, and water channelled from the surrounding tropical hills and mountains would have provided more than enough water. Amazingly enough, after having been abandoned in the 16th century, many of Machu Picchu's water systems still function, and it is said that up to 40 percent, or more of its ingenious construction consists of foundations, aqueducts, drainage channels and even cave systems below ground. The devastating floods of the summer of 2010, which damaged more than 10,000 buildings in the Sacred Valley and Cusco areas did not move a single stone at Machu Picchu. Its ancient water courses and drainage channels stood, and stand the test of time.

Stairway up through the Andene to the "Hut of the Caretaker"

"Hut of the Caretaker" with Huayna Picchu mountain in the background

The Hut of the Caretaker, another label stuck on by Hiram Bingham 100 years ago, may not have had that function at all. It may be more properly called a sentry or check point, because this is the first building of any size that greets the weary traveler who has spent 4 days on the Inca Trail. This could have been a military hut to stop any would be "gate crashers" from entering Machu Picchu without having the right credentials.

The "Funerary Rock" was clearly made prior to Inca times

The so-called Funerary Rock, next to the "Hut" was described to me by a Peruvian guide as being a place of human sacrifice. "To whom or what" I asked? "To ensure a good harvest and sufficient rain" I was told. Really, so a culture that had the Moray experimental farm, over 200 varieties of potatoes and corn, for example, which were bred to live in any possible climatic condition in the Tahuantinsuyu, massive Andene systems fed with ingenious aqueduct and other irrigations systems fed by both glaciers and rain water, still needed human sacrifice to ensure good crops? What nonsense. Unfortunately, misinformation such as this is what many of the professional guides at Machu Picchu, both Peruvian and foreign, feed their guests. The "sacrifice" idea is more likely a story made up by church officials, early on in the Spanish conquest campaign, and maintained ever since to shame the Peruvian people of Native descent into believing that their ancestors were blood thirsty heathens, which they were not.

It is far more likely that this stone, shaped out of andesite rock, which is as hard as granite, formed with steps, niches, and a flat surface that comfortably could fit a prone person, was a place of meditation, built long before the Inca, by the Hanan Pacha culture, who we will discuss in depth as we explore the whole Machu Picchu site. This is the first of many examples of intriguing stones and structures which pre-date the Inca, showing that the first constructions and occupation of the site dates back at least 4000 years, if not much longer than that.

The western side of Machu Picchu showing the amazing Andene

From this area, as an option, you can visit the amazing Inca Bridge, and/or the Inti Punku (Gate of the Sun.) The Inca Bridge is about a 15 minute walk away, along reasonably level ground, while the Inti Punku is a reasonably steep climb, along the famous Inca Trail, of about 2 miles length. Do take your time should you choose to go to the Inti Punku, taking into account the altitude you are at, and bring water!

German fans reading my first book at the starting point for the Inca Bridge

Follow the sign which is where I am looking in the photo above and you will soon see the trail entering somewhat dense brush. After this, the trail becomes more defined and winds its way around the side of the hill.

The magnificence of Huayna Picchu will be to your right

As I say, the walk to the bridge is not technically difficult, and you are protected on your right by a low wall; good thing, because the trail drops off, almost sheer by 1000 feet. This little journey is only taken by perhaps 10 percent of those that visit Machu Picchu, so you should have a tranquil time.

Safe trail, just don't look down to your right!

The Vilcanota River winds around the base of the trail at this point. The water that you see begins its life in the Andes, becomes a stream between Cuzco and Lake Titicaca, then the Vilcanota River. From the place you are watching, the Vilcanota eventually enters the Ucayali River in the Amazon basin, and in turn the Amazon River, and finally the Atlantic Ocean.

You are almost there!

Initial view of the Inca Bridge

From the vantage point of the above photo, you can see that the Inca didn't simply build a bridge, but a draw bridge using wooden planks. For security reasons, in order to restrict access to Machu Picchu, the planks could be easily removed. The only way to pass along the bridge would be to perilously climb down many feet, and then scale your way back up again; an easy target for the sentry guards who would be stationed there.

Close up of the Inca Bridge

The way back to Machu Picchu is the way you came, since it is prohibited to cross the bridge in its present state. One French tourist attempted to do so some years back and fell to his death.

At this point, you may wish to climb down the stairs near the Caretaker's Hut, or continue up and hike to the Inti Punku (Gate of the Sun.)

The latter, as earlier stated is about 2 miles, on an incline. Thus, give yourself an hour to get there, with breaks along the way.

View of Caretaker's Hut as you start the ascent

As you walk along the trail to the Inti Punku, you will probably want to keep looking over your left shoulder as Machu Picchu changes shape as you climb. The Inca Trail curves around the side of Machu Picchu mountain, and thus the angle of view of the citadel and Huayna Picchu change as you walk.

The view changes gradually as you continue the ascent

The majority of the trail under your feet is original, made up of roughly shaped paving stones of the white granite that most of Machu Picchu is composed of. The surface is not perfectly flat, but rugged enough to take your steps, as it did the Inca people and llama that crossed it hundreds of years ago.

Looking back at the cobblestone Inca Trail

Natural rock face turned into an Inca shrine

Intriguing Inca guard house you encounter along the way

Ancient shaped rock on the back side of the "guard house"

The above two photos are of a presumed Inca guard house that you pass through. It was most likely a sentry point, restricting access to Machu Picchu and also possibly a place where those that used the Inca Trail either were taxed, or made offerings to the ancient shaped stone inside. You are about two thirds of the way there, so if you still have energy, please proceed; the view is worth it!

Your arrival at the Inti Punku

The Inti Punku is regarded as having solar alignments, but their exact nature are unknown to me. Such alignments do not correspond with equinox or solstice sunrises or sunsets, as the Inti Punku is located to the south, and not east or west. However, although it is no longer in perfect condition, you can tell that it once was a closed off building, with massive trapezoidal doors front and back. This would make it a "choke point" once again controlling movement along the Inca Trail. Also, its high altitude position would make it ideal as a look out post.

The return trip to Machu Picchu will take you on average about 45 minutes, at a leisurely downhill pace.

Back at the Caretaker's Hut, you descend down from this vantage point to what is probably the main section of the oldest area of Machu Picchu. This statement is based on the fact that we find the finest stone workmanship here; clear examples of what are known as the Uran and Hanan Pacha cultures, according to Cusco based expert Jesus Gamarra. The Uran Pacha cultural period appears to have existed prior to the Inca, as in thousands of years before, and the Hanan Pacha much older than that. What distinguishes Uran Pacha construction from the Inca, is that the latter, and the Andene terraces are the clearest example, are made up mainly of field stones, and or quarried rocks of somewhat small size that were roughly assembled into walls, as are many of the buildings found at Machu Picchu. The Uran Pacha are far more refined, such that the stones fit almost exactly together, are squared off, and the surfaces smoothed.

Hanan Pacha is represented, usually, by sculpted bedrock. Often "stairs", "seats" and other flat surfaces have been shaped in the hard andesite or granite stone for no apparent reason. Often the so called stairs or steps don't lead anywhere, and the "seats" would likely have been for a more important purpose than just sitting on, taking into account the amount of time that would have been involved in making them. Also, the incredible weathering, and lack of tool marks of any kind distinguish Hanan Pacha from similar looking features made during the Inca period, which are far fewer in number.

The terms Uran Pacha and Hanan Pacha were formulated by Jesus' father Alfredo, who studied the architecture of Cusco and the Sacred Valley for many decades. These terms are his invention, and I use them here simply to distinguish the older forms of stone work from that of the Inca. As far as I know, the Gamarra's do not "own" the names, and my use of them is out of respect for their diligent research, not plaguerism. Jesus can be hired as a guide, in Cusco, the Sacred Valley and Machu Picchu, and is, as far as I am concerned, the world expert on distinguishing the difference between what the Inca made, and what those that came before did.

Doorway from the Uran Pacha period

The above doorway is a case in point; notice how the finest construction is around the door itself, and the areas above and to the left are of poorer and clearly later construction, as if repair took place. Almost all of the stone at Machu Picchu is white granite, harvested from the site itself and surrounding area, and this fact allows us to see the differences in building techniques that much more clearly.

Some people will and do suggest that the rougher work was that done during the excavations/restorations by, and after Hiram Bingham was there. But a look at photographs taken during Bingham's time, and you will see that Machu Picchu was almost intact when he stumbled over them. The lower sections are distinctly of a higher quality of masonry than the upper.

The door surround is of much higher quality than the work above it

This photo from 1911 shows distinct variations in masonry quality

Walled enclosure of the Sun Temple, with solstice window

The Temple of the Sun, which is our next major place of study, is believed to have been used by the Inca as a solar calendar, because on the solstices, at sunrise, the sun enters a specific window on the east side and strikes a line carved into a stone bedrock slab. What most guides won't tell you is that the circular temple was not built by the Inca; it's clearly Uran Pacha by the exactness of the masonry. What's more, the stone that it is enclosing is older still, Hanan Pacha. Again, what distinguishes the Uran Pacha from Hanan Pacha is that Hanan Pacha tends to be the bedrock itself, as in the case here with the Temple of the Sun.

The Uran Pacha constructions not only came after the Hanan Pacha, but, in many instances, were built next to or around the Hanan Pacha, hinting that the later builders not only recognized the earlier work, but made sure that they were not disturbed, and in fact were revered structures.

The Hanan Pacha Sun Temple rock with Uran Pacha circular wall around it

Closer look at the shaped bedrock inside the Temple of the Sun

Unfortunately, we can not clearly ascertain who the Uran Pacha and Hanan Pacha people were, or when they existed, but as you continue walking through Machu Picchu, their works show up time and again. In the 1930s, for example, Rolf Muller, professor of Astronomy at the University of Potsdam, found convincing evidence to suggest that the most important features of Machu Picchu possessed significant astronomical alignments. From these, through the use of detailed mathematical computations concerning star positions in the sky in previous millennia (which gradually alter down the epochs as the result of a phenomenon known as precession of the equinoxes), Muller concluded that the original layout of the site could only have been accomplished during 'the era of 4000 BC to 2000 BC.' The only researcher to my knowledge who has spent the bulk of his life studying the megalithic cultures that predated the Inca, and is still very much active today, is Jesus Gamarra. For more information about Jesus, and how to contact him, check out: www.theorigintour.com.

Cave system under the Sun Temple with Hanan Pacha stair system

Another scholar, Maria Schulten de D'Ebneth, also worked with mathematical methods (as opposed to historical methods which are heavily speculative and interpretive). Her objective was to rediscover the ancient grid used to determine Machu Picchu's layout in relation to the cardinal points. She did this after first establishing the existence of a central 45° line. In the process she stumbled across something else: 'The sub-angles that she calculated between the central 45° line and sites located away from it ... indicated to her that the earth's tilt ("obliquity") at the time this grid was laid out was close to 24° 0'. This means that the grid was planned (according to her) 5125 years before her measurements were done in 1953; in other words in 3172 BC.' The above is a direct quote extracted from Graham Hancock's groundbreaking work "Fingerprints of the Gods."

It is under the Temple of the Sun that we find more Hanan Pacha; a stone stairway that ends at a flat wall, and supposed evidence of a royal tomb; however, where are the royal remains? Since all of the artefacts found by Hiram Bingham and his National Geographic financed crew are now housed at the Peabody Museum at the University of Yale; perhaps only they presently know. Approximately 250 artefacts collected by Bingham, and stored at the Peabody for almost 100 years were returned to Peru in 2011, but the best specimens, perhaps as many as 35,000 are still jealously guarded by Yale University. And the skeletons dug out from their resting places, by Bingham and his team, have not been accounted for as far as I know.

Hiram Bingham discovered, and removed more than 100 skeletons from Machu Picchu. He believed that the majority of them were female, and thus immediately presumed that Machu Picchu was a sacred refuge for the Virgins of the Sun, who were the consorts of the sapa Inca, and also prepared his food and made his fine garments. However, Bingham was not a doctor, nor an anatomist, and it has been recently found that of all of the skeletons found, half were male and half female.

He spent his entire life pondering what Machu Picchu's function was, and never got to the bottom of it. However, he did remark in his book about finding the citadel, **Lost City Of The Incas**, that he believed it must have taken hundreds, if not thousands of years to build it.

Bones and skulls reputedly from Machu Picchu

The next famous place we shall visit is the Temple of the Three Windows, which is another beautiful example of Uran Pacha period construction, added onto by the Inca.

Exterior of the Temple of the Three Windows

This is more or less the entrance to the main oldest section of Machu Picchu, as you can witness from the plethora of amazing tight fitting stone work from this point. The only tools found in the archaeological record that the Inca had to shape and even sculpt stone are bronze chisels and stone hammers. Granite is a very hard rock, and even a sharpened and heat hardened bronze chisel would go dull after a few strikes on this stone, so they were clearly not the makers of the fine Uran Pacha and Hanan Pacha works.

Inside the Temple of the Three Windows; Uran Pacha

Massive granite stone, and evidence of ancient earthquake damage

From the inside of the Temple of the Three Windows, to your left, is the stairway which takes you up to the Intihuatana, the most famous and also most enigmatic stone monument at Machu Picchu, and perhaps all of South America. On our way up to it, however, you have to pass by, and enter if you wish, a most amazing little room, seen in the photo below.

The Uran Pacha period "echo room"

Some of the more astute guides at Machu Picchu will tell you to put your head into one of the niches at either end of this very well made room. If you do so, hum or make another musical vocalization of some kind. What you will notice is that certain sounds and music tones create an echo, with some even causing the room to resonate. I believe that this room was specifically designed by its Uran Pacha builders to be a meditation chamber; a place to prepare oneself prior to visiting the Intihuatana (Hitching Post) which is up an adjoining staircase.

Entrance to the Intihuatana area; Hanan Pacha

It is loosely translated to be the "Hitching Post of the Sun" and an explanation of what that in fact means is important here. On each solstice, in December and June, about the 22nd of the month, the sun stops drifting to the right on its seasonal movement, and seems to stay that way for three days, until the 25th, when it starts to move back again to the left. During this time period, it seems to "sit" in relation to the Intihuatana, as if it is fixed or tied there. In this way, the Intihuatana would tell the Inca astronomers and priests that the solstice had arrived. This was of course important for ritual reasons, as well as agricultural timing. But the Intihuatana is far more complicated and mysterious than that.

Intihuatana; looking at its eastern side

Looking at the southern side of the Intihuatana

The four corners of the Intihuatana also point to the four cardinal directions of north, south, east and west, and what is amazing, is that there are four mountain peaks that correspond to these alignments. Furthermore, on the top of each peak is an Intihuatana. Are we really to believe that the Inca went to all of that trouble in order to have an instrument that only told them what time of year it was, and when to plant or harvest food, or perform rituals directly relating to agricultural events?

I have not been able to find out from any source who made the other Intihuatanas or why they are in their exacting locations, but suspect that they, along with the beautiful stone work in the above photos was made by an older culture, the Hanan Pacha, who we know almost nothing about, except that they built megalithic works from bedrock. Such is the case of this Intihuatana, and also the one at Pisaq, another major megalithic and Inca site in the Sacred Valley area; they were not brought from another location, but are outcrops of the mountains themselves. But why was this important? The most logical answer that comes to mind is that the Intihuatana had to be fixed exactly in place, and not move, whether by human hands or earthquakes, to insure that its markings stayed true through time, indeed possibly millennia.

A somewhat more esoteric answer would be that the energy of the whole mountain, and perhaps the earth itself, was of some beneficial use to the builders and priests of the Intihuatana...

The Intihuatana as first seen by Hiram Bingham

Intihuatana facing Huayna Picchu

An even more intriguing minor aspect, in terms of a mark on the stone, is that at the upper edge corner, which faces north, is an indentation which most people are never told about. What it is, are you ready for this? It points to magnetic north. But why you, and most other people will ask, did the Inca need this? Again, the Inca probably did not construct it, and the Hanan Pacha who most likely did, must have had a reason.

Descending down the staircase, to the Huayna Picchu side of the Intihuatana, brings you to the main plaza of Machu Picchu. From here, you walk straight towards Huayna Picchu until you reach the gate which allows to to hike up the 1000 plus slippery stone steps to the top of the "Young Bird" should you be the first of 400 people to be the first each day to sign up. However, should the quota already be full for the day, or while you are pondering the 2000 stairs, have a look to your right...

A portion of the central courtyard

The "Sacred Rock" near the entrance to the Huyana Picchu stairways

The so-called Sacred Rock, as you can see in this photo, looks quite natural in appearance. It is on your right as you walk towards Huayna Picchu across the flat courtyard area. Why it has the name that it does I have never found out. But what is intriguing about it is that its shape does reflect the background; the contours do, in some ways look like the mountain in behind it. The presence of a finely made wall surrounding it does show that it was revered; and the quite tight fit of the stones could be that of the Inca, or possibly the Uran Pacha culture.

Ok, so you are either ready to ascend up to Huayna Picchu, or have been told that you are guest number 401; in either case, here is a brief snapshot of the place. The weird and awful new rule, as of 2011, is that in order to access either Huyana Picchu, or the Temple Of The Moon, located around the back of Huayna Picchu, you have to buy an extra entrance ticket. And foolishly, in my mind, is the fact that this must be done prior to entering Machu Picchu itself; it has to be purchased "on line," and at least the day before!

Magnificent Huyana Picchu

What many people don't realize is that Huayna Picchu is not simply a mountain. The reason why there are stairs, all 2000 of them, that lead you to the top is the fact that there is a large complex of buildings encircling the summit, with enough Andene to feed many cliff top inhabitants. In fact, the top of Huayna Picchu was so well provisioned, that several Inca, or even earlier people, could have happily lived up there without ever having to come down!

Buildings and Andene on top of Huayna Picchu

But what would have been its function? The obvious, but most typical and boring explanation would be that it was a military lookout for detecting the presence of possible invaders, but, who would they have been? Local natives from the nearby jungle? Hardly. As I have already said, the bulk of the Inca period construction at Machu Picchu most likely occurred during the reign of the Inca Pachacutec in the 15th century, and by that time this area was tightly under control of the Inca, and their sizable military forces.

More likely, it was a place where spiritual advisers or even astronomer priests lived; the two quite possibly being one and the same. Contrary to the western world and it's compartmentalization of roles and careers, in the Inca scheme of things, cosmology and religion were very much interlinked. The sun, Inti, was the physical manifestation of the divine source, Viracocha; the moon, Quilla (or Killa) was the female aspect, and different star systems formed the shapes of animals; llama, frog, serpent, etc.

One of the caves that you climb through on your ascent

One of the last flights of steps before the top

The way up is worth the effort, because at the top you get an incredible panorama of the entire Machu Picchu complex. And it is from here that you also see that Machu Picchu was designed in the shape of an enormous condor, its head facing west (upper right hand corner.) The official entry and exit route, the Inca Trail, can be seen in the upper left hand section of the photo.

Machu Picchu as seen from the top of Huayna Picchu

Condor eye view of the great city shaped like...a condor!

Strange, possibly ancient Hanan Pacha style sculpted stone

View of the sacred Vilcanota River as it winds around Huayna Picchu

If you still have energy, and are still adventurous, follow the sign from the top of Huayna Picchu that leads you down the back side. Through a series of trails, stone stairs, and ladders you make it half way down the mountain to the Temple of the Moon; most likely a place of pilgrimage for the Virgins of the Sun.

The beginning of the way down to the Temple Of The Moon

One of the wooden ladders on the way down to the Temple of the Moon

And yet another wooden ladder!

Possibly Inca period buildings near the Temple of the Moon

Probable Hanan Pacha style construction on the right

The author on a Hanan Pacha "throne" in the Temple of the Moon"

View from the "throne"

Astonishing workmanship inside the Temple Of The Moon

The masonry here is immaculate; perhaps the best that exists in the Machu Picchu area, and also shows us that the earlier cultures were here before the Inca; the Uran Pacha constructing the tight fitting rock wall and enclosure structures, and the Hanan Pacha the megalithic single stone works, such as the seat that I sat on. There are also agricultural terraces here, enough, like at the peak of Huayna Picchu, to feed quite a few people. So it too may have been a place where devotees could have lived for extensive periods of time without having to leave back to the main Machu Picchu area.

The trip down from the top of Huayna Picchu takes about an hour, but this beautiful area is also accessible from the main courtyard area of Machu Picchu.

Again, the walking time down is about an hour, but for the return trip give yourself one and a half, or even two if it is raining.

The walk, or should I say hike back to the main area, to your right, is less challenging than the way down from Huayna Picchu, but not easy by any means. Remembering that you are still at about 8,000 feet or so of altitude, your heart sounds out the upward effort; take your time, and observe the wonderful "Hawaiian climate" plants like bamboo and orchids along your path.

Stone walkway back to Machu Picchu

View of Machu Picchu proper from the trail leading from the Temple of the Moon

Looking down on the way back up

The trail that you are now following winds back up stone staircases, some carved directly into the bedrock, and along pathways that end up at the eastern side of Machu Picchu's buildings and squares. The most interesting place in the area to go next, as we follow our clockwise tour pattern, is the Temple of the Condor.

Approach to the Temple of the Condor, seen top center in this photo

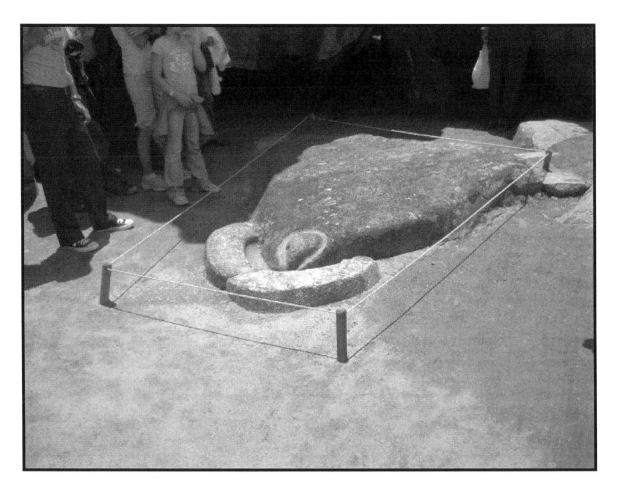

Temple of the Condor

The path which takes you there is on the eastern side of the entrance to Huayna Picchu, right next to the "Sacred Rock." It takes you through several narrow pathways, in between mainly Inca period construction. Then, you will see a sign that guides you down into the Temple of the Condor. The tear drop shape in the main stone is said to represent the head of the condor, and the two curved stones the white ring that encircles its neck. Also, the wall directly behind the shaped "head" stone appears to be the wings, facing left and right. The head is directed towards the east, and thus to the sunrise.

Close up of the "head and neck" of the Hanan Pacha Temple of the Condor

It's function? Again, most sources say "ritual purposes" which is as vague as one can be. I honestly have not been able to find real details as to what the function of this place was during Inca times, and before the Inca got here. In some ways that is good, as mysteries prompt one to "dig" deeper.

In the Inca belief system, three animals were and are of prime importance, the serpent (snake), puma and condor. This coincides with their notion of three levels of consciousness; the subconscious, conscious and super conscious. The subconscious is represented by the snake (wisdom), the puma is the conscious mind, and the condor the super conscious.

What you may have noticed by now is that the three presumed oldest structures at Machu Picchu, as in the Temple of the Sun, Intihuatana and Temple of the

Condor contain, in the immediate vicinity, the oldest of the constructions, as in Uran and Hanan Pacha. It could well be that these three areas were the only ones that existed prior to the Inca, and that the citadel was built around them.

Back towards the entrance we must now walk...

The sad trip back to the entrance gate...

And so now we leave Machu Picchu, having not seen everything, nor revealed every secret of the place, but have learned much more than the average tour of the area gives. And as a teaser for future study, Machu Picchu is of course not the traditional, ancient name for this area. Hiram Bingham chose to name it after the mountain on which it resides, or more specifically, the one that rises to the south side, and along which the Inca trail clings. The traditional name for this sacred space is Yllampu, which in Runa Simi, also known as Quechua, means "The Resting Place of the Gods." Quite appropriate I think...

To end this book, I have included in the following pages photos taken during the excavations by Hiram Bingham, around 1911 to 1913, as well as photos from the 1950s, before Cusco and Machu Picchu were as easy to get to as they are today. Note the differences in building techniques, giving you further indication that the Inca were the last great builders at Machu Picchu, but not the first.

Possibly the first photo ever taken of Machu Picchu

Hiram Bingham on the left with some of his crew

As the jungle was slowly cut away, revealing the majesty

Early view of the Temple of the Sun

Massive blocks in the Temple of the Three Windows

Western flank of Machu Picchu with some unknown guy!

Machu Picchu in 1911, covered in vegetation

As they were found, with the Intihuatana in the background

Temple of the Three windows interior

Templ of the Sun with Huayna Picchu in behind

Another view of the Temple of the Sun

Unidentified building showing amazing masonry genius

The author with the Intihuatana all to himself...bless you Machu Picchu

I have now, at the time of finishing this, 10 books to my credit. All are available as e-books at: www.brienfoerster.com, www.hiddenincatours.com, www.hiddenincavideos.com, and www.amazon.com Brien Foerster. Covers of each of my other 9 books can be seen on the following pages.

Thank you so much for purchasing and reading this; I hope t has brought you insight, joy, and that Machu Picchu was and is a highlight of your life. I personally never tire of visiting this beautiful space, and am often available to give tours there. If you are interested, check out www.hiddenincatours.com.

Blessings, Brien

The Inca are known around the world for having developed the largest civilization in all of the Americas. With a standing army of at least 100,000 highly trained troops, how was it possible for a group of 160 Spanish soldiers of fortune to defeat them? This book endeavors to explain that, as well as the origins of the Inca, their social makeup, and their proud history.

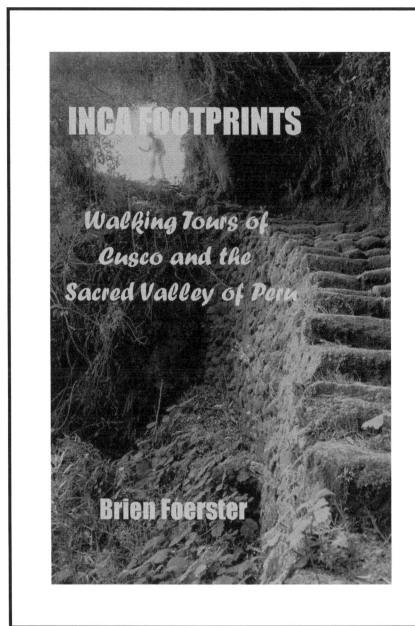

I wrote this book as the result of not finding anything similar to it in Cusco, or anywhere. Cusco and the Sacred Valley are full of ancient megalithic stone remains and structures, many of which are far older than the Inca, and this fact is not explained, and in fact not known by many of the guides and tour companies there. This book is the result of 5 years of on the ground research by me, Brien Foerster, and contains so many photos, that the book acts as a virtual tour of the whole area.

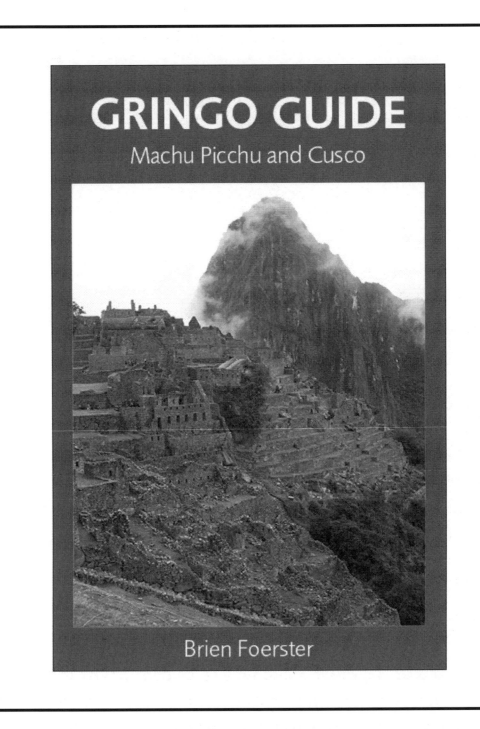

A guide to Cusco and Machu Picchu; strategic tips on how to prepare for a trip to Peru, and how to get around, economically, without the need of tour guides or the ability to speak Spanish. I have also included insights into the true ages of the megalithic structures of the Cusco area, including Machu Picchu. Many of them are far older than the Inca…

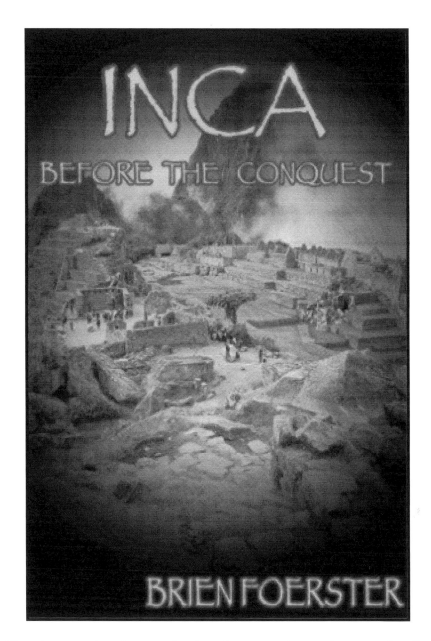

The Inca civilization evolved out of what is now Tiwanaku, south of Lake Titicaca in Bolivia. From there they founded the city called Cuzco, high up in the Andes of Peru, which served as the capital city of an expanding world which at its prime, in the early 16th century, was the largest civilization in the Americas. The step by step expansion of the Inca, from the 12th century in Cuzco, to the apex of their existence is covered in this book, Inca: Before The Conquest. Meant as a guide for travelers to Peru, and also for students of history, this book is a detailed account of the Inca world, with many photos, all condensed in a portable and very readable format.

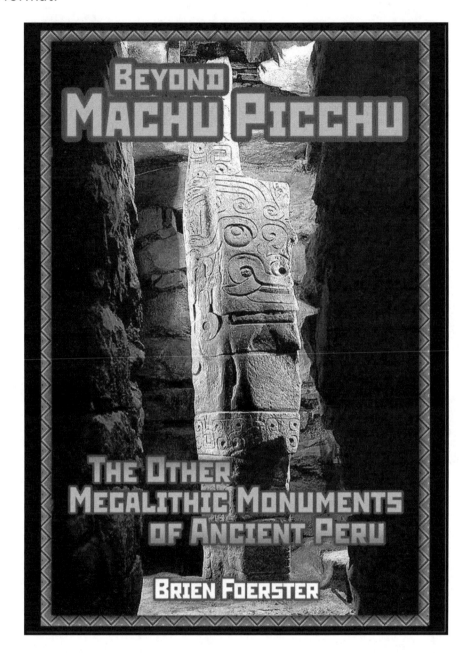

The majority of visitors to Peru vist Cuzco and Machu Picchu, and that is all, not even knowing, in some cases, that there are amazing megalithic structures and mysteries all over the country, from north to south, and west to east. The Inca and their accomplishments were and are amazing, but so too are the grand works of the Moche, Chimu, Chachapyas and others. The WHO? you may ask. In this book I cover all of the major megalithic sites of Peru, and give directions on how to find them easily.

Amongst the least understood of ancient megalithic sites in South America is Tiwanaku, located about 12,500 feet in elevation near Lake Titicaca, Bolivia. And even less is known about Puma Punku, which is in fact part of the Tiwanaku complex, and displays levels of stone shaping craftsmanship that can barely be recreated today. Who built these amazing places, when, and why? Brien was featured in an hour long special on Ancient Aliens TV, season 4 discussing both places...or are they one and the same?

Hawaii: The majority of books written about Hawaii, in my experience, contain little information about the Hawaiians themselves, and especially about their history prior to the arrival of Captain James Cook. I lived in Hawaii, and learned the oral traditions from the Hawaiians themselves. Two major waves of migration occurred there, separated by more than 1000 years. And it was the interaction, battles, and melding of these two peoples that make up who the Hawaiians were to become. Where did the Hawaiians come from? What is a Kahuna? Who were the Hawaiian monarchs? And how did the US "acquire" this chain of islands? This book answers these questions, and many more.

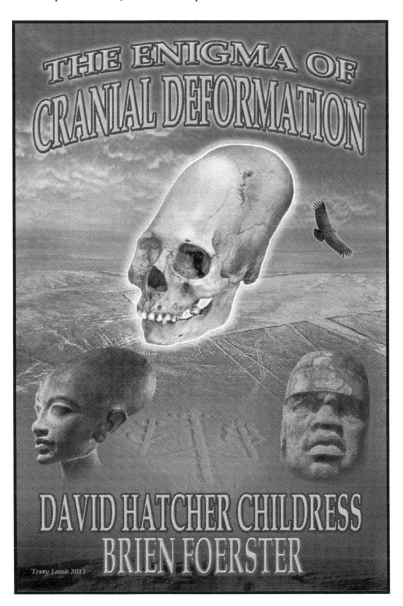

Lost Cities author Childress tackles the enigma of worldwide cranial deformation along with Canadian-Peruvian anthropologist Foerster. In a book filled with over a hundred astonishing photos and a color photo section, Childress and Foerster take us to Peru, Bolivia, Egypt, Malta, China, Mexico and other places in search of strange elongated skulls and other cranial deformation. As incredible as it seems,

Childress and Foerster discover that cranial deformation was practiced on nearly every continent by special groups who believed they were imitating their highly advanced ancestors. This is a mind-blowing trip into the strange past of humans on planet Earth.

The people of the Pacific known by most as "Polynesians" remain a mystery to scholars and the public alike as to their origins. While most academics in the fields of archaeology and anthropology strongly insist that they exclusively came from south east Asia, other researchers, and the oral traditions of the people themselves often differ with this opinion.

The presence of red hair, called "Ehu" in Hawaii and "Uru Kehu" in some of the ancient and present populations suggest connections, in the distant past, with sea farers from coastal Peru, especially the Paracas, to account for this.

The famous explorer Thor Heyerdahl was insistent that there were ancient connections between Peru and the Pacific Islands, and this book attempts to solve this riddle, without delving into Celtic or other possible European ancestry. Come explore the possibilities through science, wind directions, sea currents, sculpture, and oral traditions.